Tomer Ganihar Raving in the Desert

This catalog is dedicated to my mother, Diana.
Special thanks to the Levadi family.

　Tomer Ganihar

Tomer Ganihar

Raving in the Desert

Contemporary Arts Center
New Orleans

Tomer Ganihar
Raving in the Desert

Contemporary Arts Center, New Orleans
Lupin Foundation Gallery

January 15 – March 27, 2005
Contemporary Arts Center, New Orleans

Winter 2006
Museum of Art Ein Harod, Israel

Organized by David S. Rubin
Curator of Visual Arts
in cooperation with Pamela Auchincloss/
Arts Management

The exhibition and exhibition catalog have been generously supported by:

Elizabeth Firestone Graham Foundation

Lyn and John Fischbach

Topor Family Foundation

G.A.B.Y. Foundation

Israeli National Lottery Council for the Arts

Catalog design and production:
Michael Gordon Studio, Tel Aviv
printed and bound in Israel

All rights reserved © Copyright 2005
Contemporary Arts Center, New Orleans
All images © Copyright Tomer Ganihar

Library of Congress Cataloging-in-Publication Data

Ganihar, Tomer, 1970-
Tomer Ganihar : raving in the desert / [authors, David S. Rubin, Daniel Belasco].
p. cm.
"Organized by David S. Rubin, Curator of Visual Arts, in cooperation with Pamela Auchincloss/Arts Management. Exhibition itinerary: January 15-March 27, 2005, Contemporary Arts Center, New Orleans" --T.p. verso.
ISBN 0-9702670-8-8 (alk. paper)
1. Photography, Artistic--Exhibitions.
2. Raves (Parties)--Israel
--Pictorial works--Exhibitions.
3. Photography--Israel--Exhibitions.
4. Ganihar, Tomer, 1970- --Exhibitions.
I. Rubin, David S., 1949- .
II. Belasco, Daniel, 1965- .
III. Pamela Auchincloss/Arts Management.
IV. Contemporary Arts Center
(New Orleans, La.)
V. Title. VI. Title: Raving in the desert.
TR647.G42 2005
779'.995694--dc22

2004024880

Table of Contents

	Foreword	7
	Acknowledgments	9
Daniel Belasco	**Land of the Rave**	11
David S. Rubin	**L'Chaim: The Photographs of Tomer Ganihar**	15
	Catalog	23
	Biographical Notes	61

Foreword

One of the most profound expressions any artist can undertake is that of successfully capturing the heart of one's culture. Creating a true representation of where a people are—intellectually, spiritually or physically—seems to leave a lasting impression on the observer. Tomer Ganihar's exhibition *Raving in the Desert* is one that succeeds on all three counts. With camera in hand, Tomer isolates moments where masses engage in both personal and communal expression. As I respond to his imagery, I am reminded of the transcendental feelings I have when listening to music, first discovered in my youth and most of which found its path to immortality through festivals such as Woodstock and the Isle of Wright. I suspect that "events" such as these are markers for my generation. These celebrations were highly influential on those of us growing up in the 1960s and 1970s, as they steered many of us in new directions along our paths to maturity.

It comes as no surprise that Tomer's generation has found its own significant markers. Unlike the events that defined the lifestyle of my generation, however, the raves in Tomer's photographs are of a religious tone. Through photography, Tomer attempts to document these events from the vantage point of young Israelis, for whom the encounters are closely connected to ancient Jewish mysticism. The desire to find a sense of spiritual belonging, as exhibited by the Israeli ravers, is indeed a universal one. In many cultures, past and present, people seem to have a common need to find transcendent moments when being apart from the body brings a tranquility that feels separate from everyday experience. Interesting enough, this serenity comes through very physical exertion. Raves are not a passive experience. One does not simply escape into the "beat" of the music. Rather, one is consumed by music's cyclical nature. Writing about an experience that is so physical and spiritual, in fact, seems to have taken me back to where I started.

On behalf of the Contemporary Arts Center, I wish to thank curator David Rubin for his commitment to this project. Tomer's photographs excited him from the moment he saw them, and I share with him this enthusiasm. I also am grateful to Pamela Auchincloss and Paul Rodgers for their part in coordinating this exhibition and catalog, and to the Contemporary Arts Center staff for their continued hard work and dedication. Lastly, thank you Tomer Ganihar for sharing your beautiful, uplifting vision with the people of New Orleans.

Jay Weigel

Executive Director
Contemporary Arts Center, New Orleans

Acknowledgments

It has been about two years since I first came into contact with Tomer Ganihar's world. While making the rounds through the Chelsea galleries in New York City, I walked through the doors of Paul Rodgers/9W to encounter an exhibition that left me breathless and awestruck. I remember being particularly entranced by the photograph *God is in Our Clubs*. As I cast my eyes over the figures swirling amidst soft golden light, I instantly understood that this was a powerful, religious image. Perhaps in part due to my own Jewish heritage, I connected what I was seeing with the abstract paintings of Mark Rothko and Barnett Newman, whose work—through it's radiant colored light—has always made me think about the eternal light above the pulpit in the Jewish synagogue.

When I visited the gallery a year later, Paul Rodgers remembered my enthusiasm for Tomer's art, and mentioned that there was interest brewing in seeing it documented through a publication. I am grateful to Paul for inviting me to be involved in the project, which includes this handsome catalog and an exhibition of eighteen large-scale photographs. I am equally indebted to Pamela Auchincloss, who has collaborated with the Contemporary Arts Center in coordinating the exhibition and tour, and in producing the catalog.

Raving in the Desert has been a team effort on many levels. Ms. Auchincloss has been expertly assisted by Christopher Saunders, James Morrison, and Nicole Wong; Mr. Rodgers has been assisted by Yesenia Cardona, Regina Abramovich, and Shira Agmon; and at the Contemporary Arts Center we are fortunate to utilize the skills of C.C. Campbell-Rock, Administrative Assistant; Kate Cromwell, Curatorial Assistant; and Johnny King, Chief Preparator.

I also wish to thank Jay Weigel, CAC Executive Director, for warmly embracing this project from the very beginning.

Additionally, gratitude is extended to Daniel Belasco, for enriching our understanding of Tomer's art through a vivid and insightful essay on the Israeli rave culture, and to Michael Gordon, for his beautiful catalog design.

Financial support for *Raving in the Desert* has been contributed by the Elizabeth Firestone Graham Foundation, Lyn and John Fischbach, the Topor Family Foundation, The G.A.B.Y. Foundation, and The Israeli National Lottery Council for the Arts. We are all so grateful for your dedication to sharing Tomer's photographs with the people of New Orleans and, through the publication, with audiences around the globe.

Finally, it has been a delight getting to know Tomer Ganihar and to share in his vision. L'Chaim Tomer! May your flame continue to burn brightly throughout the years ahead.

David S. Rubin

Curator of Visual Arts
Contemporary Arts Center, New Orleans

Land of the Rave

Daniel Belasco

A rave, simply stated, is an underground, informal, and sometimes illegal, dance party organized around high-tempo, repetitive electronic music. Sensations of wordless music, light, and psychedelic art wash over dancers, reaching deep into some internal, primordial rhythm and propelling them for hours. This sound-body fusion generates a powerful sense of togetherness and joy, far greater than that created at a typical club or concert. Thus the rave kid's banner "PLUR" (peace, love, unity, respect) professes optimism and liberation, a postmodern multicultural updating of the Sixties hippie mantra "make love, not war." Public displays of polymorphous sensuality are never taken lightly by the powers-that-be, however. Mainstream culture has presented raves as weirdly subcultural, if not downright threatening and subversive. An episode of the popular teen program *Beverly Hills 90210* from 1991 shows the danger of a rave when a central character goes to one and is promptly drugged by his girlfriend with ecstasy, rave drug of choice, and goes crazy for the night. At stake in all of this, from the utopian claims of ravers to the puritanical response of authorities, is the vitality of the largest international youth culture trend to have emerged since hip-hop. The image of thousands of young people dancing for days in abandoned warehouses or outlying lots from Pasadena to Pakistan looks a lot like a revolution.

    Raves in Israel are no exception, as they display the commonplace bliss, drugs, and relentless digital music. Yet Israelis also have made raves their own, not surprisingly for a nation that has always adored and reviled its sense of uniqueness. Though raves originated in Europe in the 1980s, many Israelis first encountered them on the beaches of Goa, a former Portuguese colony on the west coast of southern India. Popular since the 1960s for Western travelers and dropouts, Goa is a favorite destination for young Israelis on walkabout after serving their mandatory military service. Fleeing the tensions and stresses of

Daniel Belasco is a former staff reporter for The Jewish Week *and is currently working toward his doctorate in art history at the Institute of Fine Arts, New York University.*

terrorism and occupation, they flock to unguarded spiritual places from the mountains of Patagonia to the beaches of Thailand. In Goa, Israelis discovered all-night parties, where disk jockeys set up on the beaches and birthed trance, fusing eastern and western elements with stronger beats and melodies than other rave music, dripping psychedelic ornaments and spacey computer-generated sound effects. Since the late 1980s, Goa has been the Israeli mecca of trance liberation. Enterprising deejays and promoters brought the musical magic back to their homeland in the early 1990s, and thus the Israeli trance scene was born.

Initially, raves in Israel were granted police permits and sponsored by hopeful anti-drug organizations. But as fears of drug culture spread, authorities began making arrests at the multi-day festivals that attracted thousands. In response, leftist activists organized raves because they considered the rave to be a new form of civil disobedience. Caught amid Israel's ongoing cultural civil war, trance may have achieved its greatest visibility and public debate in Israel in the late 1990s, which, not coincidentally, was the last time of relative peace. At "Give Trance a Chance," over 30,000 thronged Yitzhak Rabin Square in Tel Aviv to dance and protest the government crackdown on raves. Today, fears of terrorism have significantly reduced the number of large public gatherings. Free movement is more curtailed than ever, and the trance scene has been thrown up against the backdrop of the hawkish government of Ariel Sharon.

Trance music still predominates at Israeli clubs, but foreign deejays, once enamored with the unrestrained enthusiasm on the Tel Aviv dance floors, are coming in smaller numbers. Record companies specializing in Goa trance music are now among the largest independent labels in the country, and trance albums are Israel's biggest musical export. In spite of the music's popularity, however, raves have gone back to being an underground culture. Diehards must negotiate anonymous emails, remote meeting points, vague maps, and stern checkpoints in order to arrive at a rave. Once there, they discover a smaller scene that remains committed to its ideals. At an Israeli rave, the moment of truth occurs at sunrise, when the break of light reveals the countenances of the anonymous bodies heaving together in unison. If the magic holds, then the unity of night can be carried forth into the next day, and the day after that, until the next rave.

For those who have never experienced an Israeli rave, it might be tempting to draw parallels with European raves and American outdoor festivals like Burning Man. But in Israel, the raves are imbued with numerous additional layers of spirituality. The dancing can be related to "shuckling," the back-and-forth swaying of orthodox Jewish men in prayer. Trance music also evokes *niggunim,* repetitive sung Hasidic melodies that promoted impassioned spirituality to combat the modernization and secularization of Judaism. The fact that many trance festivals are held on Friday nights or during Jewish holidays precludes participation by observant Jews. Instead, the raves present the opportunity for secular Israelis to create personal rituals to connect to the sublime aspects of Judaism. Held in remote forests, beaches, and deserts, raves bring urban Israelis closer to the beauty of nature, to the very land dreamt of by modern Zionism founder Theodor Herzl in Vienna at the end of the 19th century, and fought for still today by the Israeli army.

Israeli raves also embody longings for cultural and spiritual unity with other people. By linking their Jewish spiritual ecstasy to that of other cultures, as in gospel music and whirling dervishes for example, they aspire to overcome the particularism of being a member of "the Chosen People." Many musical elements of trance are taken from Indian and other eastern music, adding a non-Western beat that transcends the European culture that still influences a now diverse Israeli society, one that includes Jews from North Africa, the Middle East, India, Russia, Ethiopia, Europe, and the Americas, not to forget the marginalized Palestinians, Druze, and Bedouins that make up twenty percent of the population.

Raves are an expression of independence of mind and body for mainly secular, middle class Israelis. In the past four years, Palestinian suicide bombers and the Israeli government response of building a separation wall have wiped out nearly all hope for a peaceful solution for Israel's security. Beset with a faltering economy, international criticism, threat of bombings, and disillusionment from their participation in a society that kills in their name, young Israelis have struggled to find an identity. They wish to be international yet are also stubbornly nationalistic, contemporary yet irresistibly connected to a Biblical sense of place. Israelis fed up with occupation and all the "isms" have turned to trance raves for a new consciousness that envisions peace with neighbors and celebrates the value of the individual. Raves in Israel send a powerful message. In a nation so conflicted and militarized, the longing for "PLUR" is far more political than in the United States, which enshrined the pursuit of happiness in its founding document.

On balance, any written description of a rave risks reducing it to a series of clichés about togetherness, oneness, and liberation. We are fortunate to have Tomer Ganihar's photographs, which more accurately transmit the vibrancy of the scene to a distant and unfamiliar audience. Taken at raves and other dance happenings in Israel from 1996 to 2003, Tomer's photographs capture the many contradictions at play. Some of his images, in particular *The Parting of the Red Sea* **p. 35** and *Holy Rave* **p. 47**, may be compared to a powerful scene from Arnold Schoenberg's modern opera *Moses and Aaron.* Performances of the unfinished masterpiece climax at the end of Act II. The Israelites, anxiously waiting the descent of Moses from Mount Sinai, grow fearful and impatient. To sooth them, Aaron provides the Golden Calf to mitigate their loss of faith in God. Moses descends Mount Sinai, observes the orgiastic frenzy, and smashes the tablets of the law.

Mass worship of the sensual, be it the Golden Calf or electronic music, is said to be deviant behavior that threatens the future of the collective. As the Calf will prevent them from accepting one God and reaching the Promised Land, so will the rave disrupt the serious business of security against the Arab "threat." Unlike the Bible, which describes the fulfillment of God's promise with the bloody entry of the Israelites into Canaan, Moses and Aaron remains unresolved. There is no Act III. There are only unanswered questions. What will save and preserve Israel: adherence to an invisible God, the political expediency of the state, or the human necessity of pleasure? An Israeli rave is an ephemeral utopia, the wellspring of dreams, and, as a poet wrote in the dark year 1937, "in dreams begin responsibilities."[1]

[1] Delmore Schwartz, *In Dreams Begin Responsibilities,* New York: New Directions, 1978.

L'Chaim: The Photographs of Tomer Ganihar

David S. Rubin

Perhaps living in a war zone makes one particularly prone to possessing an optimistic yearning for global harmony like that which characterized the hippie rituals of the American Peace Movement of the late 1960s. At least for Israeli artist Tomer Ganihar, that period in our cultural history produced the seeds of the similar rave-culture lifestyle that he adopted in the early 1990s. Born in 1970, just three years after the Arab-Israeli War of 1967 and the concurrent "Summer of Love" in San Francisco, Tomer was being groomed for the military from his very beginnings. The son of an Israeli attorney and an American mother who had worked in Hollywood before moving to Israel, Tomer was raised in a middle-class Tel Aviv suburb where children are expected to enter the army when they reach eighteen. Accordingly, he volunteered in 1988 to serve full-time in a Special Forces division of the Israeli army, but soon after basic training, he broke his back when equipment collapsed during a drill. As a result, he was transferred first to an intelligence unit and eventually to the Israeli version of the Secret Service. Although he was now spared the overtly physical rigor of combat, Tomer found military existence stressful and depressing. He remembers the unofficial military credo as being something like "We are not here to enjoy ourselves, we are here to work and suffer," a doctrinaire attitude that he likens to the rigid viewpoints of Orthodox Judaism.[1]

Tomer's eye-opening, life-changing introduction to rave culture occurred in 1990, while he was still serving in the military. During a weekend leave, he attended a trance party in the woods near a lake at Galil Heights, in northern Israel. At this event, between ten to twenty people joined in a circle and danced to trance music, a hypnotic style of electronic music that eschews lyrics and can thus function as a universal language. According to Tomer: "Trance music was first heard in the late 1980s in Goa, an old Portuguese colony in the south of

[1] Tomer Ganihar, in conversation with the author, New York City, March 12, 2004.

India. Tourists from Europe played it on a basic computer at the time. Trance is the 'illegal' son of electronic music of the '80s, then led by the German experimental group Kraftwerk. At mystical Goa, people shared their new tracks with each other and played together. That fact, along with ecstasy, the new drug from London that allowed people to dance for days, gave trance the appeal of music for the masses."[2]

Tomer readily embraced his first rave as an uplifting "alternative to the despair of the army, violence, chauvinism, and an aggressive society."[3] He also recognized that, on a personal level, trance music was for him the equivalent of what Beatles music had been for his parents. In Israel, global pop culture had made its way into society in increments. Although the Beatles were banned from preforming in Israel in the 1960s, their music had become acceptable by the 1970s and Tomer's parents played it constantly when he was a youth. Peace-loving songs like "All You Need is Love," "Across the Universe," and so many others by the Beatles symbolized "that there is more to life than war and Holocaust, that the West suggests more than just fear and violence and boring Zionist manifestoes." Tomer recalls, "When I saw the smile on their faces while they listened to that music, I understood that music means freedom. I treasure that memory today. Trance music is my freedom, my Beatles."[4]

Another way of coping with the pressures of military life for Tomer was the creative outlet of photography. Knowing that he had the army darkroom at his disposal, Tomer brought his camera to his second trance party, an event that he remembers as being "all light and hope."[5] Seeking to capture "the light and the dance," he took pictures and, back on the military base, proceeded to develop them in the darkroom, a place where he "could create beauty working with reality" and that reminds him of a Catholic confession booth where "all the secrets are revealed."[6] Inspired by the alchemical nature of a radiant image gradually emerging on photographic paper, Tomer remembers holding his first positive as being rather momentous—it made him feel "connected to light, to nature, to grace, to life."[7]

In Israel, veterans of the army receive a small stipend to travel to a place of their choice, anywhere in the world. Although the monetary

[2] Tomer Ganihar, e-mail to the author, July 24, 2004.

[3] Ganihar conversation, March 12, 2004.

[4] Tomer Ganihar, e-mail to the author, July 23, 2004.

[5] Ibid.

[6] Ganihar conversation, March 12, 2004.

[7] Ganihar e-mail, July 23, 2004.

amount is nominal, Tomer took advantage of this opportunity and added his own savings. After leaving the army in 1992, he traveled to Goa, India—the birthplace of European rave culture. A popular tourist spot for Israelis, Goa was home to small primitive raves, much like the one Tomer had attended in Galil Heights. According to Tomer, visitors to Goa brought the rave culture to Israel around 1990. Israeli youth would learn of the gatherings by word of mouth and, by the mid-1990s, attendance at the raves had grown to around 30,000 people. In addition to these outdoor festivals, clubs where deejays would spin trance or house music had also gained in popularity.

After returning home to Israel, Tomer settled into a low-rent rooftop living space in the south of Tel Aviv, and continued photo-documenting the rituals of his new lifestyle. Although drugs like ecstasy were available, he found that he could not function on them and instead chose only to drink vodka. For Tomer, the "real drug" was photography and the marvel of "something completely new . . . raving was a new way of diving into Judaism without forgetting your roots and doing it in your own way."[8]

Many of Tomer's early photographs were taken at the Cinema Allenby Club in Tel Aviv. Tomer has described the clubs as being "sort of temples, up-to-date and autonomous halls of assembly that enable a pure release of all the aggressions that exist outside. In these halls it is possible to escape. In these halls the rhythms are the most right, the stunning lighting the most beautiful, the video films on the walls are the most appropriate psychedelia . . . A public ecstasy."[9] His account is certainly applicable to his photographs *God is in Our Clubs* **p. 27** and *The New Synagogues* **p. 29**, where club dancers appear as anonymous revelers united by color, light, and swirling movement. The artist recalls that at Cinema Allenby Club he "experienced moments of holiness . . . as well as hair-raising, hellish moments. Lots of love, lots of overwhelming loneliness. Here people don't only escape from confrontation; here they simply find new and amazing aesthetical ways of arriving at a temporary cease-fire with it. And in the air above you and beneath you and inside you, pulses the decisive sensation that all this is happening now. At the right time. In the right place. And that is photography.

[8] Ganinar conversation, March 12, 2004.

[9] Tomer Ganihar, in *Tomer Ganihar: We Shall Live to See*, Tel Aviv Museum of Art, 2000, 14.

10
Ibid.

11
Lawrence Fine, *Safed Spirituality: Rules of Mystical Piety, The Beginning of Wisdom,* Ramsey, New Jersey: Paulist Press, 1984, 7.

12
Tomer Ganihar, e-mail to the author, July 12, 2004.

13
Ganihar, e-mail to the author, July 25, 2004.

And this is my aim, to prove that God is present everywhere."[10]

The concept of God's omnipresence is not a new one in Jewish thought. It can be traced to the teachings of the ancient Kabala, which have particular significance for Tomer because he was raised in a neighborhood that is known for its Kabalistic heritage. According to the Kabala, divinity exists in two realms—a spiritual reality and a material one. As Lawrence Fine has explained, "Not only does everything in the material world *mirror* a spiritual reality above, but everything in creation is invested with divine vitality or abundance from the *Sefirot* [the aspects of God]. There is a continuous flow of divine nourishment and blessing from one realm of existence to the other, endowing all things in the lower world with life. In order to express this relationship, the Kabbalah uses the image of a cosmic chain in which everything is linked to everything else. All the elements of existence—from the most hidden to the most visible—are intimately and inextricably bound to one another. All things trace their roots back to the inner recesses of the Source of all being, *'Ein-Sof* [the unknowable aspect of God]."[11]

Another Jewish tradition that Tomer embraced in his early club photographs is that of Kaddish, the customary prayer of mourning for the dead. Photographed the day after a suicide bombing in a nightclub that took the lives of twenty Jewish youths, *Kaddish (The Day After a Bomb)* **p. 33** shows a solitary anonymous figure, seated in a bar and bathed in rapturous light from above. According to the artist, "I showed here that my generation could mourn in its own fashion in a bar, at night, alone with one's thoughts and a bottle of beer."[12] Tomer titled the photograph after Allen Ginsberg's poem of the same name, which was written in memory of the poet's mother. In calling the poem *Kaddish,* Ginsberg essentially expanded upon the traditional Jewish mourning ritual, reshaping it within the context of contemporary everyday life. With Ginsberg as his role model, Tomer followed suit photographically and, serendipitously, today he lives in the very building where Ginsberg wrote *Kaddish.*[13]

In 1998 and 1999, following visits to annual raves in the forest at Latrun, Tomer produced a number of images in which intense natural light is the dominant force. In *The Parting of the Red Sea*[p. 35], piercing bolts of light remind the artist of God's separating the waters for Moses; and in *Faces to the Moon*[p. 41], golden light suggests Kabalistic pollination—that is, divinity flowing from the spiritual realms to the masses. As Tomer so eloquently puts it, "In the photographs I took, I captured the light that sang at those unique events. In every negative, and in every picture, this very light is caught: the light that illumines this stirring, effervescing period that floods and guides all my sleep and my rest and my consciousness."[14]

Within an art historical context, it is significant to note that light perceived as a spiritual entity has been a subject for Jewish and non-Jewish artists alike. In the late 1940s, for example, the American Jewish artist Barnett Newman began painting abstract stripes, which he called "zips," that have been related to the Kabala and described as "rays of light piercing through the coloured (sic) grounds."[15] According to John Golding, Newman titled the earliest of these paintings *Onement* as a play on atonement, which he turned into "at-onement," referring to "Atonement and the events of Yom Kippur, for the Kabbalists a time for meditation on the messianic secret, on the coming which symbolizes rebirth and the possibility of a new and radiant life."[16] The power of moonlight, on the other hand, was a fascination for the devoutly Christian nineteenth-century artist Caspar David Friedrich. According to Sabine Rewald, the German Romantic painter once told visitors to his studio that "his many moon-lit pictures would bring him, after his death, 'to the moon' instead of to 'the beyond.'"[17] Friedrich painted several paintings of people gazing at the moon, such as *Two Men Contemplating the Moon* (1819, Gemäldegalerie Neuemeister, Staatliche Kunstsaamlungen, Dresden), in which two evening strollers pause before the brilliant luminescence of the moon and the nearby planet Venus, which "to the deeply religious Friedrich . . . were emblems of the divine."[18]

While all of Tomer's photographs reveal his Kabalistic interpretation of the universe, his images are also informed by the cultural and political changes that have influenced his generation of Israelis. When they were children, Tomer and his peers were visually

[14] Ganihar, in *We Shall Live to See*, op. cit., 26.

[15] John Golding, *Paths to the Absolute: Mondrian, Malevich, Kandinsky, Pollock, Newman, Rothko, and Still*, Princeton, New Jersey: Princeton University Press, 2000, 197.

[16] Ibid., 195.

[17] Sabine Rewald, *Caspar David Friedrich: Moonwatchers*, New York: The Metropolitan Museum of Art, 2001, 9.

[18] Ibid., 30.

19
Ganihar conversation, March 12, 2004.

20
Ibid.

21
Ganihar e-mail, July 12, 2004.

22
Ibid.

23
Ganihar, in *We Shall Live to See*, op. cit., 26.

deprived and at the same time propagandized by television. Only one station was available and its purpose, according to the artist, was "to poison us to become soldiers."[19] By the late 1980s, however, Israel had become open to foreign influences. With Yitzhak Rabin heading a left-wing government at the time, "MTV was introduced, the new age had arrived, and young people began to take positions in the economy."[20] With images and sounds of international pop stars like Madonna now gracing television screens, it became increasingly difficult for youth to justify the requirement of Orthodox Judaism that women shave their heads and be segregated from men during worship and other rituals. Tomer's acceptance of a feminist viewpoint on these issues is celebrated in photographs like *Raving in Jerusalem*[p. 49] and *Equal Praying*[p. 39], which were taken during the Shantepee Festival of 1999. His focus in the former work is on "the radiating, mesmerizing feminine beauty that stares shamelessly into your eyes."[21] In the latter, he gleefully documents both genders dancing and praying together in public, activities that traditionally "required separation between both men and women."[22]

Tomer often refers to the subjects of his photographs as the "new Jews," because he believes that a new "Jewish atmosphere" has arisen among Israeli youth. According to the artist, "The spirit has always existed here, we've always been a geographical intersection for great questions and great answers. And today there's the strange and marvelous feeling that it's all happening again. . . . Tens of thousands of young people, searching for meaning, all of them gathering together, celebrating this tremendous trinity of nature-music-seeking . . . a Jewish atmosphere. Except that now the atmosphere wears new colors, correct angles, new faces. A new aesthetics. An aesthetic of ancient Jewish content renewing themselves and raising their heads with pride."[23]

Such aesthetics, one that emphasizes light, color, and movement as vehicles for expressions of celebration and joy, may easily be compared to that introduced in France nearly a century earlier by Matisse and the Fauves. In Matisse's *The Dance* (1909, Museum of Modern Art, New York), five nude women are shown dancing in a circle, with the rhythm of the dance accentuated by bold curving outlines and a corresponding brilliant palette. Matisse's well-known *"joi d'vivre"* outlook on how we should ideally spend our time is echoed, but demonstrably amplified in Tomer's *Hebrew Tribe #2* **p. 43**, where colored light envelops revelers engaged in what the artist describes as his favorite subject, "mass ecstasy."[24] Additionally, whereas Matisse's vision at the time was secular, Tomer never forsakes religious connotations and connections to the past—here, by invoking the designation of "tribe" and, in other examples, by revealing that the Israeli rave experience incorporates and revamps age-old observances, such as the pilgrimage that is taken during the springtime holiday Shavuot. In *Holy Land X* **p. 45**, Generation X ravers are shown carrying a primitive Jewish star during the agricultural festival where worshippers traditionally commemorate God's giving of the Torah to Moses by dressing in white and bringing fruits and bread to the synagogue as gifts to God. Compositionally, the processional movement in the photograph recalls Italian Old Master depictions of Christ carrying the cross on the Road to Calvary by such artists as Giotto or Simone Martini.

In photographs produced since the turn of the millennium, Tomer has increasingly called attention to the natural elements. In addition to the ever-present light, other forms of matter—including earth, wind, and water—encompass individuals and groups in womblike fashion, thereby representing God's presence. As if it is a protective mystical force, dust sheathes an anonymous figure in *Crossing Over* **p. 37**, a photograph that was taken at Mount Herzl overlooking Jerusalem on the morning of the last day of the millennium. In *Wings* **p. 55**, one of the only images that Tomer shot in black-and-white, a dancer is shown swirling amidst white sheets flailing in the air. Here God's power is equated with whirlwind motion and the flapping of bird wings, ultimately alluding to freedom. And in *Fragments of Light* **p. 59**, taken during a break from dancing at a Tel Aviv beach, three men are nurtured by a gust of sparkling light and droplets of water, as if they have been blessed by a higher power with a communal "baptism."

When asked to name his favorite artists, Tomer cites Marc Chagall, because, "he proved that religion can fly in the sky like a

[24] Ganihar e-mail, July 12, 2004.

bird," Max Ernst, because, "he painted the dream," and Weegee, because he dared in his photographs to document the truth, that is, "he never faked and he had balls."[25] It is significant to note here that Tomer's preferences reveal an interesting polarity, in that Chagall and Ernst are at the opposite or complementary end of the spectrum than Weegee. Chagall and Ernst embraced the spiritual realms in their art, equating them with fantasy and the unconscious. Weegee, by contrast, was a documentary photographer who directed his camera towards all aspects of the real world, be it life or death, with no holds barred. In Tomer's photographs, a strange and beautiful reconciliation occurs between both of these arenas, as the material and spiritual converge to form a harmonious marriage. It is as if Tomer has come to realize that our intensified cognition of spiritual beauty need not be set apart as a form of surreality, hyper-reality, or even virtual reality. Rather, if we open our eyes and ears a bit, we might be better able to accept the Kabalistic notion that divinity exists within every form of materiality, and view amplifications of consciousness as meaningful extensions of our everyday lives.

[25] Ganihar e-mail, July 23, 2004.

Catalog

All works courtesy of Paul Rodgers/9W Gallery, New York

Becoming a Generation. 1996, C-print mounted on aluminum. 48 × 72 in / 120 × 180 cm

God is in Our Clubs. 1996, C-print mounted on aluminum. 48 × 72 in / 120 × 180 cm

The New Synagogues. 1996, C-print mounted on aluminum. 72×48 in / 180×120 cm

The Day After (My Neighborhood). 1997, C-print mounted on aluminum. 48×72 in / 120×180 cm

Kaddish (The Day After a Bomb). 1997, C-print mounted on aluminum. 72×48 in / 180×120 cm

The Parting of the Red Sea. 1998, C-print mounted on aluminum. 48×72 in / 120×180 cm

Crossing Over. 1999, C-print mounted on aluminum. 48 × 72 in / 120 × 180 cm

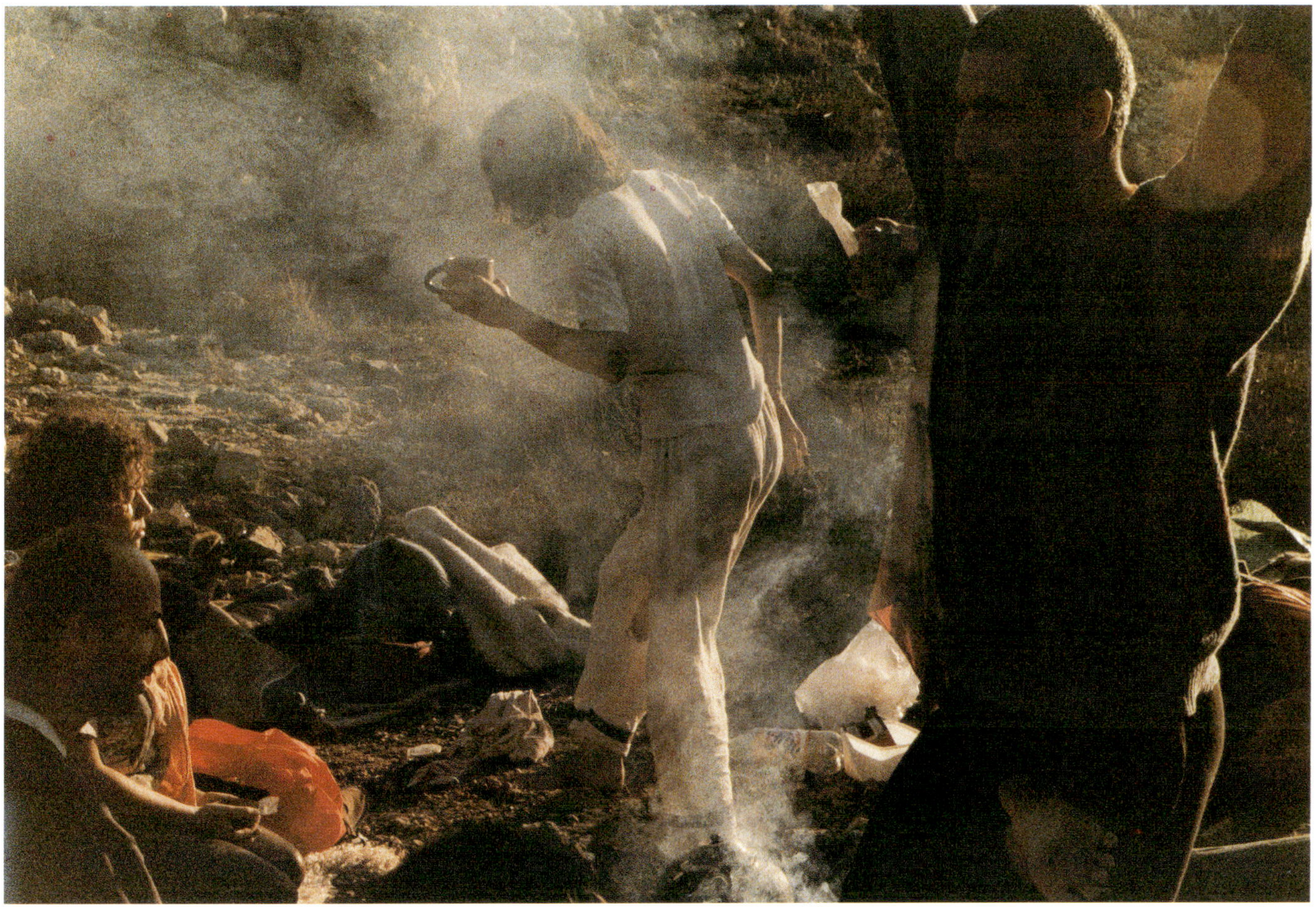

Equal Praying. 1999, C-print mounted on aluminum. 48 × 72 in / 120 × 180 cm

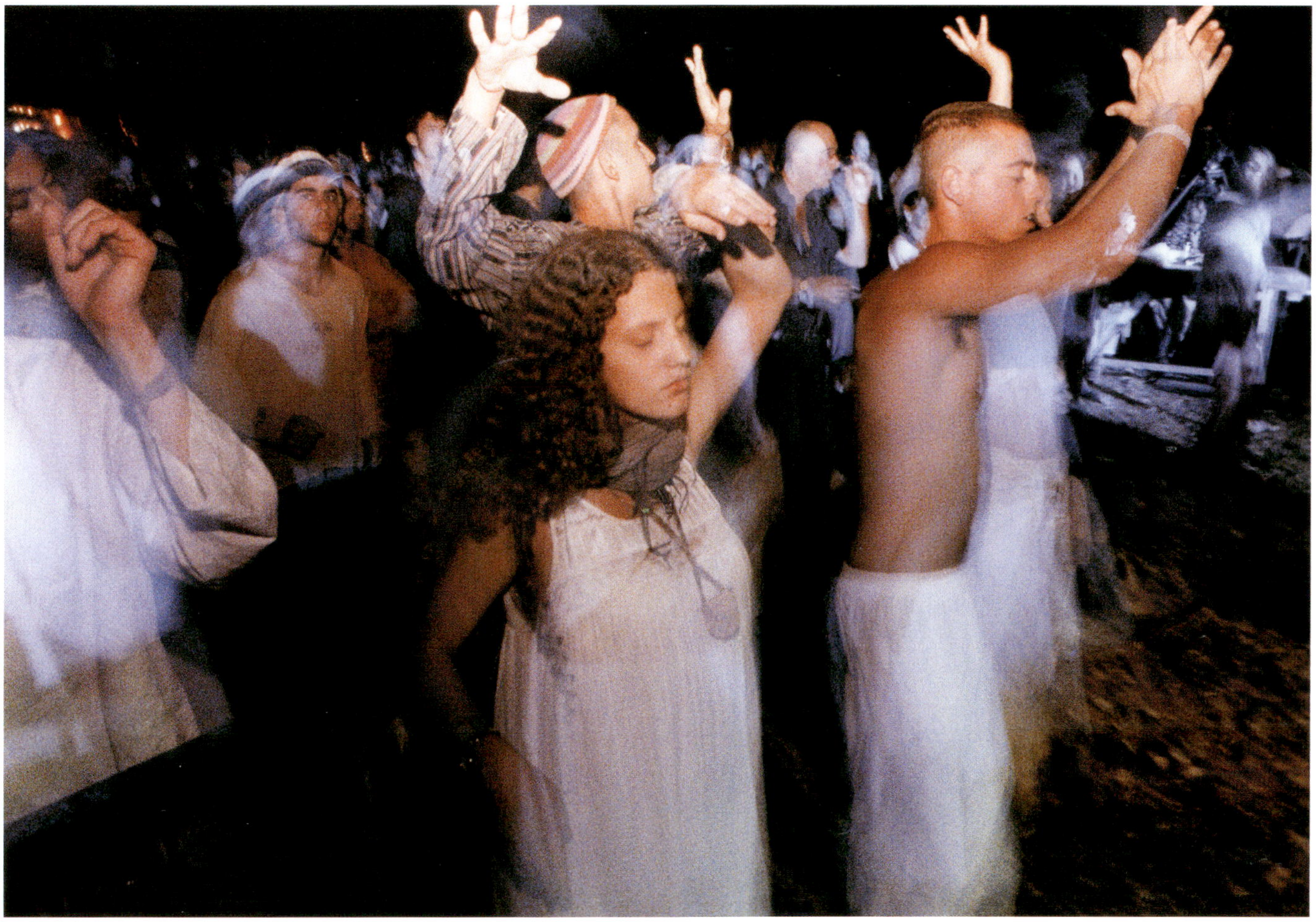

Faces to the Moon. 1999, C-print mounted on aluminum. 72 × 48 in / 180 × 120 cm

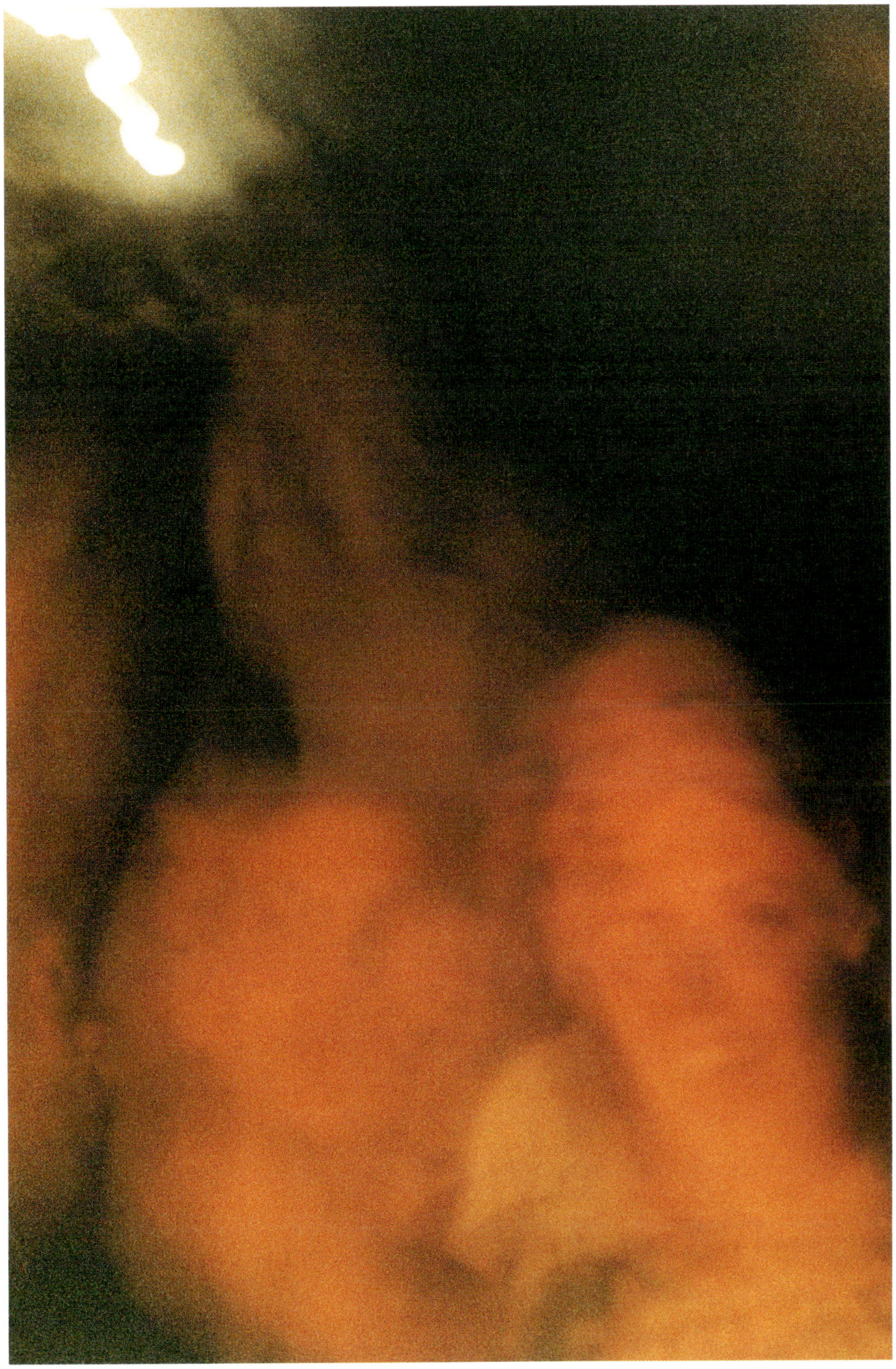

Hebrew Tribe #2. 1999, C-print mounted on aluminum. 48×72 in / 120×180 cm

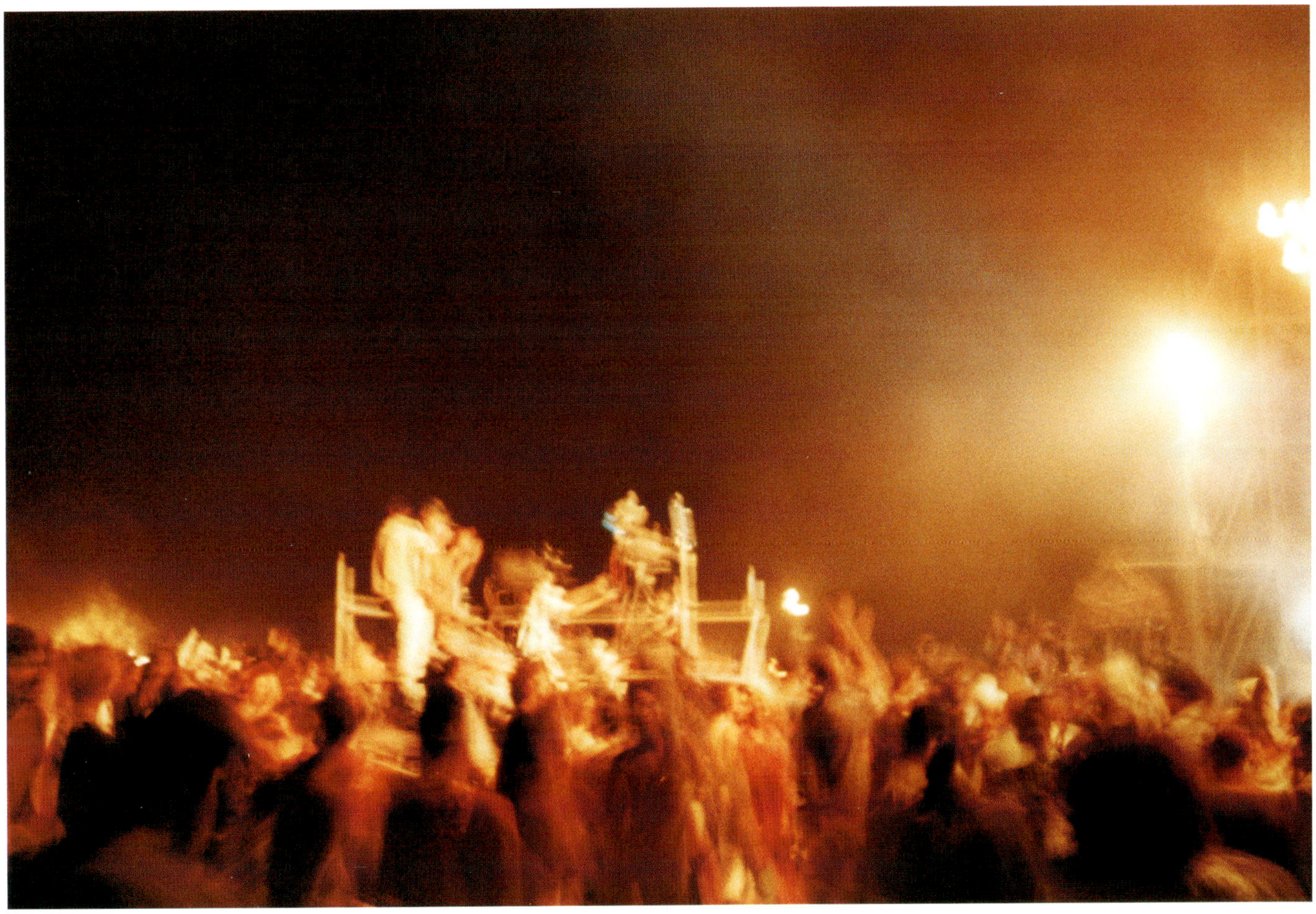

Holy Land X. 1999, C-print mounted on aluminum. 48 × 72 in / 120 × 180 cm

45

Holy Rave. 1999, C-print mounted on aluminum. 48×72 in / 120×180 cm

47

Raving in Jerusalem. 1999, C-print mounted on aluminum. 48×72 in / 120×180 cm

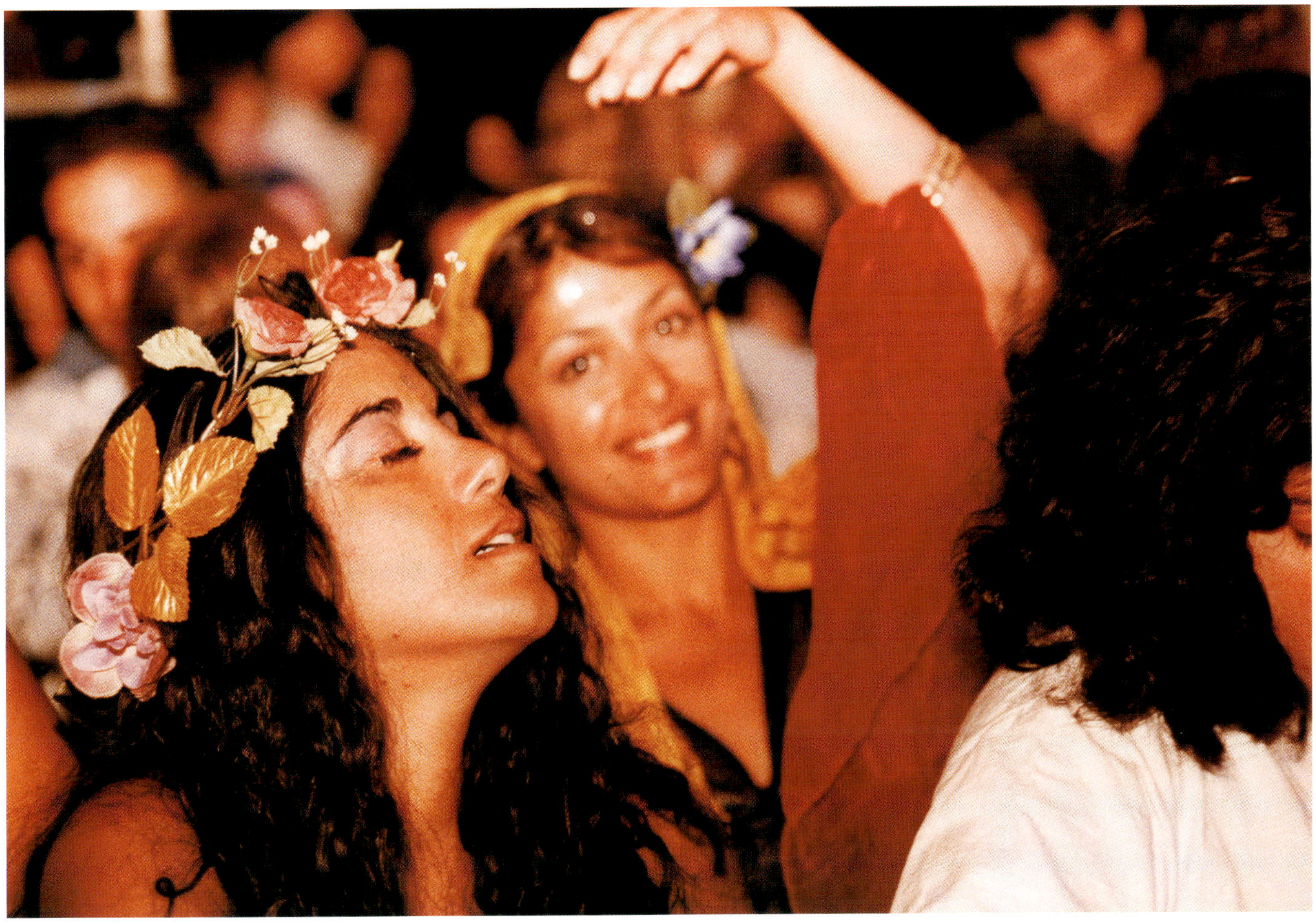

Raving in the Negev Desert. 2000, C-print mounted on aluminum. 48×72 in / 120×180 cm

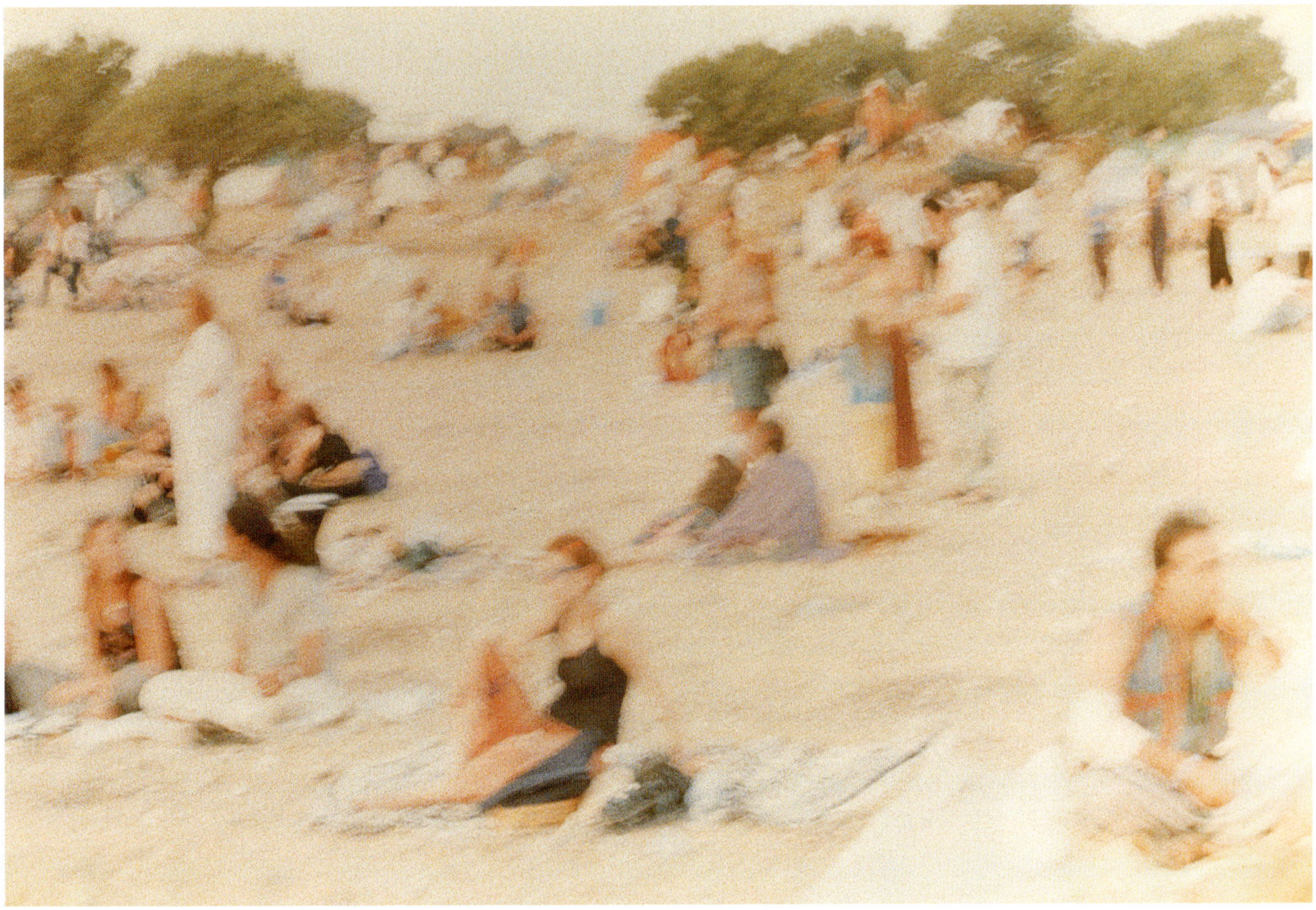

We. 2001, C-print mounted on aluminum. 48 × 72 in / 120 × 180 cm

Wings. 2001, C-print mounted on aluminum. 48 × 72 in / 120 × 180 cm

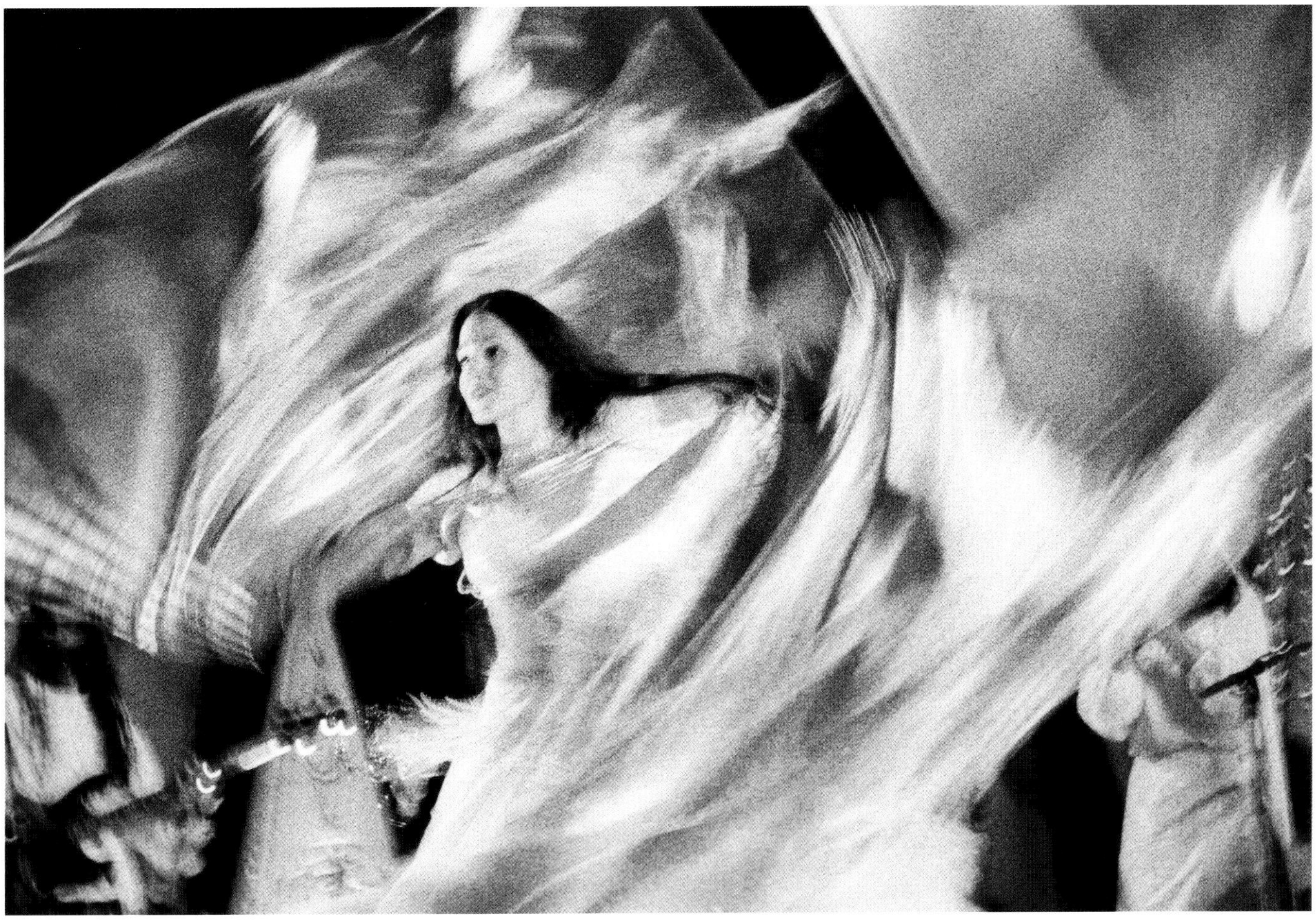

The Woods. 2003, C-print mounted on aluminum. 48 × 72 in / 120 × 180 cm

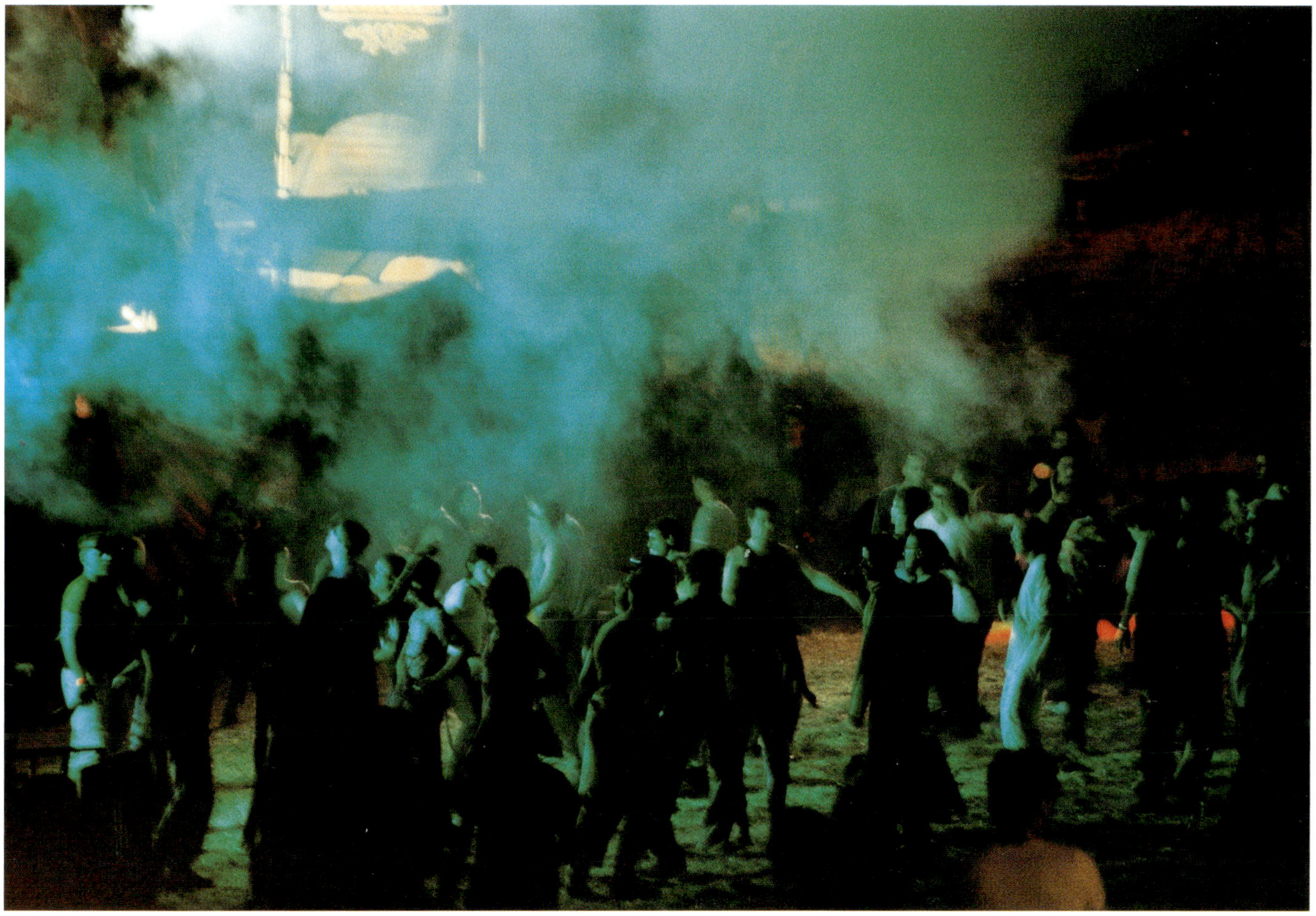

Fragments of Light. 2003, C-print mounted on aluminum. 48 × 72 in / 120 × 180 cm

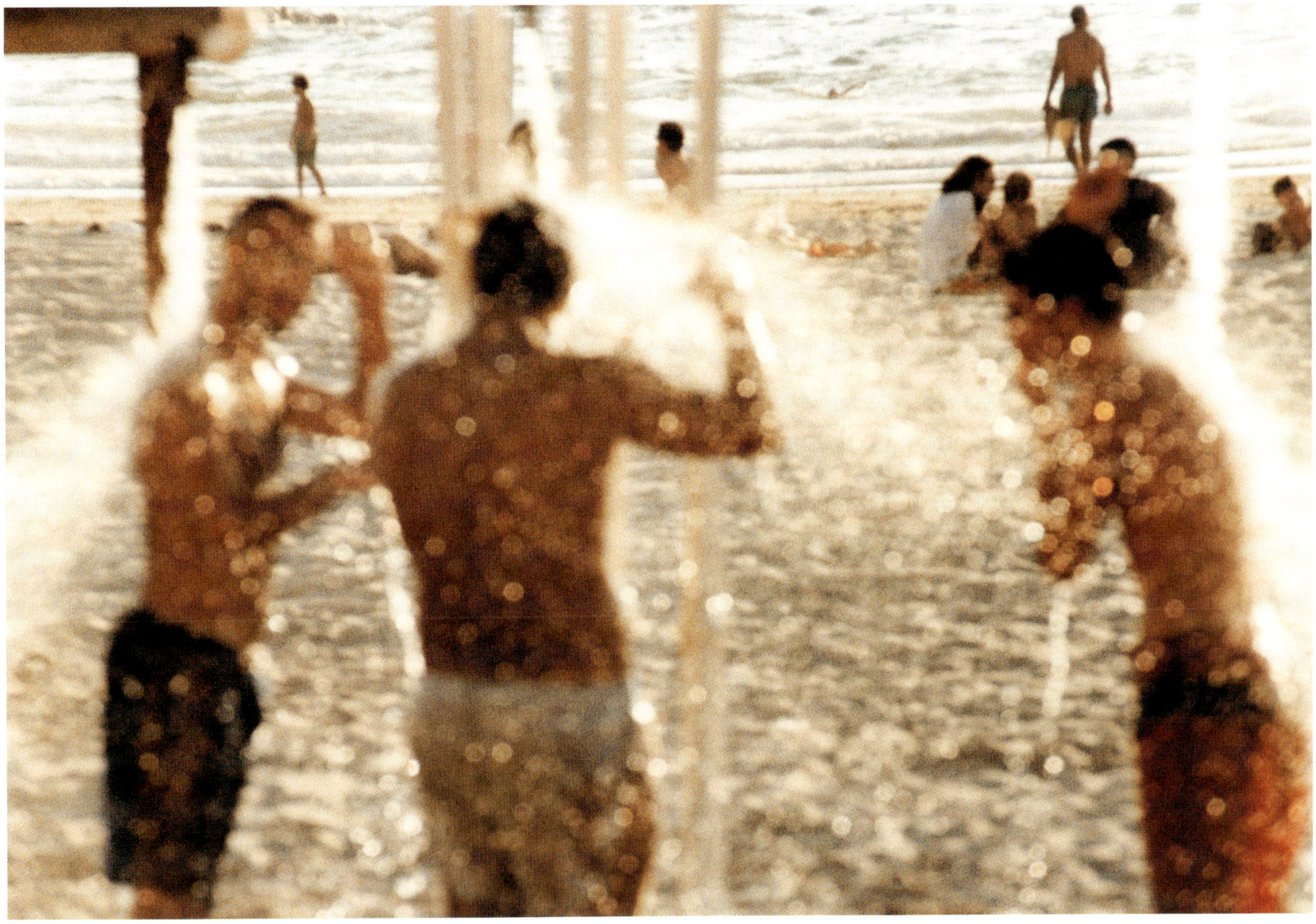

Tomer Ganihar

Born 1970, Tel Aviv, Israel

Education

Self-Taught

Awards

- 1998 – Yehoshua Rabinovitz Foundation Writing Grant
- 1997 – The President's Residence Prize for Young Artists

One-Person Exhibitions

- 2005 – Contemporary Arts Center, New Orleans
  - – Paul Rodgers/9W, New York
- 2003 – United Nations Headquarters, New York
- 2002 – Paul Rodgers/9W, New York
- 2000 – Tel Aviv Museum of Art
- 1998 – Azrieli Center, Tel Aviv
  - – Chelouche Gallery, Tel Aviv
- 1997 – Limbus Gallery, Tel Aviv

Group Exhibitions

- 2003 – *Recent Acquisitions,* The Jewish Museum, New York
- 2001 – *Spunky,* Exit Art, New York
- 2000 – *Views from Israel,* Gallery of Contemporary Art, San Francisco
- 1999 – *90th Anniversary of Tel Aviv,* Tel Aviv Museum of Art
- 1998 – *Urban Touch,* Camera Obscura, Tel Aviv

Bibliography

- Bach, Deborah. "In Raves, An Israeli Finds His Woodstock." *The New York Times*, February 9, 2003.
- Goldman, Julia. "All the Rave." *Jewish Week* (New York), November 15, 2002.
- Kaufman, Fred. "Goings on About Town," *The New Yorker*, November 11, 2002.

**Contemporary Arts Center
Board of Directors**

Brent Barriere
Denise Berthiaume
Sydney J. Besthoff III (Emeritus)
Jane Boettcher
Edward Butler
Patricia Chandler (Emeritus)
Serafina Vivian Charbonnet
Thomas B. Coleman (Emeritus)
Richard W. Cryar
Bennett Davis
Bonita Day
R. Allen Eskew (President)
Vaughn Fauria
Tracey Flemings-Davillier
Aimee Freeman
Sandra Freeman (Emeritus)
Tripp Friedler
Patricia Fullmer
Nan Wallis Galloway
Luba Glade (Emeritus)
Campbell Hutchinson
Beth Lambert
Henry Lambert
Martha Landrum
Elly Lane
Sally Lapeyre
Jim Lestelle
Lory Lockwood
Philip Manuel
Myron Moorehead, M.D.
Barbara Motley (Emeritus)
Jeanne Nathan (Emeritus)
Sunny Norman (Emeritus)
Graham M. Ralston
Françoise Billion Richardson
Katherine Saer
Milton W. Seiler, Jr., M.D.
Ronald Sholes
Michael J. Siegel (Emeritus)
Stephen L. Sontheimer (Emeritus)
Ann Cox Strub
John J. Sullivan
Sally Suthon
Sandra Trout-Wilson
Melanee Gaudin Usdin (Ex-Officio)
MK Wegmann (Emeritus)
Joel Weinstock (Emeritus)

**Contemporary Arts Center
Visual Arts Committee**

John Barnes, Jr.
Ron Bechet
Mark Bercier
Denise Berthiaume
Kathy Cacioppo
Gerald Cannon
Bonita Day (Chair)
Iva Gueorguieva
Sally Heller
Theresa Herrera
Frahn Koerner
Juan Laredo
Delaina Leblanc
Robin Levy
Lory Lockwood
Mary Jane Parker
Joseph Pearson
Anastasia Pelias
Karoline Schleh
Maxx Sizeler
Ann Cox Strub
John J. Sullivan
Sandra Trout-Wilson
Kathy White

**Contemporary Arts Center
Staff**

Luisa Adelfio · Director of Development
Morgan Aldrich · Frontline Staff
Chris Britt · Production Assistant
Stephanie Brownlow · Assistant Director of Development
C.C. Campbell-Rock · Administrative Assistant for Visual Arts
Kate Cromwell · Curatorial Assistant
Richard Douvillier · Front Desk Manager
Annie Fleetwood · Finance Assistant
Neil Fuselier · Director of Production
Dave Gajee · Systems Administrator
Manney Garcia · Frontline Staff
Glenn Gruber · Associate Director for Finance and Operations
David Hardegree · Operations Manager
Wanda Harvey · Janitorial Services
Gail Hill · Administrative Assistant, Executive and Performing Arts
Deborah Jacobs · Janitorial Services
Reese Johanson · Special Events Coordinator
Steve Kalra · Frontline Staff
Johnny King · Chief Preparator
Marie Lamb · Education Director
Vera Lester · Membership Coordinator
Tim McCoy · Box Office Manager/Frontline Supervisor
Shelley Middleberg · Director of Sales
Daniel Ostrav · Frontline Staff
Jacquelyn Phillips · Finance Assistant
David S. Rubin · Curator of Visual Arts
Nathalie Schroeder · Frontline Staff
Aimee Smallwood · Associate Director
Gigi Taylor · Grants Coordinator
Jessica Troske · Frontline Staff
Melissa A. Weber · Marketing Coordinator
Jay Weigel · Executive/Artistic Director
Jeff Zielinski · Technical Director

Visual Arts programs for 2004-2005 are made possible with the support of Dorian M. Bennett, Inc.; The Sydney & Walda Besthoff Foundation; Le Chat Noir; Eskew + Dumez + Ripple; E. Eean McNaughton Architects; Mulate's Restaurant; Cole Pratt Gallery; Arthur Roger Gallery; and Wisznia & Associates, AIA.

The Contemporary Arts Center is supported in part by a grant from the Louisiana State Arts Council through the Louisiana Division of the Arts and the National Endowment for the Arts; by a Community Arts Grant made possible by the City of New Orleans as administered by the Arts Council of New Orleans; and by The Sydney & Walda Besthoff Foundation; Zemurray Foundation; Goldring Family Foundation; Eugenie and Joseph Jones Family Foundation; and the Downman Family Foundation. Additional support contributed by ChevronTexaco Corporation and The Helis Foundation.